APPROACH TO FLOURISHING

A GUIDE TO ACHIEVING FINANCIAL GREATNESS IN THE 21ST CENTURY

KING SMARTY

Table Of Content

Introduction

In a world that is continually developing, where potential open doors are plentiful yet challenges are various, the mission for monetary significance has turned into a yearning shared by a lot of people. Welcome to "Approach to Flourishing: a guide to achieving financial greatness In the 21ST century." This book is your compass, directing you through the complex territory of monetary achievement, strengthening, and the quest for a day-to-day existence that is both plentiful and significant.

As you stand at the limit of your journey, it's essential to perceive that quite possibly the most intense resource you have is your age. In the year 2023, at the youthful age of 16, you will enjoy an unrivaled benefit: the force of youth. This power isn't to be undervalued, for it can shape your way of life in ways you cannot yet completely handle. The choices you make, the propensities you develop, and the information you get during this significant stage will lay the groundwork for the existence you're bound to lead.

The Benefit of Beginning Young

Imagine a seedling that is tenderly supported and given adequate daylight, water, and care. Over the long run, that seedling changes into a powerful oak tree, its underlying foundations profound and solid, its branches venturing high out of sight. Essentially, your childhood is your sustaining period when your psyche is open, your energy is limitless, and your ability to learn and adjust is unrivaled. You have the advantage of time to try, fizzle, learn, and attempt again.

Beginning young means you get the opportunity to intensify your endeavors. The choices you make today can possibly increase throughout the long term, prompting remarkable development. Whether you're taking a stab at monetary freedom, looking to gather riches, or seeking to turn into a tycoon, the propensities you foster presently will determine the direction of your prosperity.

Exploring the Advanced Landscape

The world you're venturing into is not normal for anyone else. Innovation has changed ventures, opening new entryways and disturbing customary pathways. The web has democratized data, empowering you to gain and procure abilities from the solace of your own space. Business has moved from a far-off dream to a feasible reality for anyone with a flash of development and assurance.

This book is intended to be your buddy as you explore this powerful scene. Every part will furnish you with important bits of knowledge, down-to-earth procedures, and noteworthy advances that line up with your yearnings. From monetary proficiency and schooling decisions to business ventures, speculation, and keeping a solid balance between fun and serious activities, we'll cover a range of themes that are crucial for your joyful journey.

Holding onto the opportunity

As you read through the pages of "Approach to Flourishing," recollect that each recommendation, each story, and each idea is intended to enable you. The path to monetary significance is certainly not a simple one, yet it is without a doubt . With responsibility, constancy, and the right outlook, you can conquer obstructions, adjust to changes, and emerge as a guide for progress.

Whether you come from a foundation of overflow or misfortune, whether your objectives are humble or daring, remember that the journey is basically as significant as the objective. Embrace the course of development, gain from each insight, and develop a feeling of strength that impels you forward.

Your journey into monetary significance starts now. The force of beginning young is your benefit, and this book is your aide. As you turn the pages, ingest the insight shared, and imagine the existence you want, realize that you are making a functional stride towards creating a future that isn't simply monetarily prosperous but also profoundly satisfying.

Embrace the force of beginning youth and let the excursion to monetary significance unfold. Your experience starts here.

Chapter 1

Building Areas of strength

As you continued looking for monetary significance, the excursion started with building a powerful establishment. This establishment isn't just about monetary procedures; it's tied in with developing the right outlook, setting clear targets, and fostering the personal qualities that will drive you forward. How about we investigate the vital components of this primary part?

Putting forth Clear Objectives and goals

Objectives are the compass that directs your journey. They provide you with an internal compass and motivation. To define successful objectives:

Be Explicit: Clearly characterize what you need to accomplish. Whether it's monetary freedom, beginning a business, or putting something aside for a significant purchase, particularity assists you with remaining on track.

Make Them quantifiable. Measure your objectives so you can keep tabs on your development. This makes it more straightforward to remain alert and make changes when they are important.

Guarantee They're Attainable: While aggressive objectives are exemplary, they ought to likewise be sensible. Survey your ongoing conditions and assets to guarantee your objectives are achievable.

Significance Matters: Adjust your objectives to your qualities and long-term desires. At the point when your objectives resonate with your basic beliefs, you're bound to remain committed.

Set Time spans: Lay out cutoff times for your objectives. Having a time frame makes you feel the need to get moving and assists you with arranging your activities in a similar manner.

Fostering a Development Outlook

A development outlook is the conviction that your capacities and insight can be created through exertion, learning, and diligence. This attitude enables you to embrace difficulties, gain from disappointments, and consistently get to the next level.

Embrace Difficulties: Consider difficulties as potential open doors for development. Rather than staying away from them, embrace them as opportunities to acquire and foster new abilities.

View Exertion as a Way to dominance. Understand that achievement requires difficult work and steady exertion.

The more you put resources into learning and practicing, the better your results will be.

Gain from Difficulties: Rather than considering inability as a last decision, treat it as a significant example. Investigate what turned out badly, adjust your methodology, and utilize the experience for your potential benefit.

Look for Feedback: Productive analysis gives bits of knowledge to progress. Welcome input from guides, friends, or associates, and use it to refine your techniques.

Be Enlivened by Others' success. Allow others' accomplishments to move you as opposed to cause you to feel undermined. Perceive that their achievements are a demonstration of what's conceivable through devotion and exertion.

Persevere Despite Misfortune A development mentality energizes flexibility. When confronted with misfortunes, keep up your assurance and stay zeroed in on your objectives.

Developing Discipline and Deferred Satisfaction

Monetary significance frequently requires discipline and the capacity to defer quick compensations for long-term benefits.

Put forth boundaries: Distinguish your most significant monetary objectives and allot your assets, including time and cash, likewise.

Construct Sound habits: Lay out schedules that help your objectives. For example, saving a part of your pay routinely or reliably and putting resources into your schooling

Practice Postponed delight: Train yourself to oppose incautious choices and momentary joys that can obstruct your drawn-out monetary advancement.

Make Responsibility: Share your objectives with somebody you trust, whether it's a companion, relative, or coach, who can assist in considering you responsible.

The Significance of Deep-Rooted Learning

In the quick-moving universe of money and self-awareness, nonstop learning is your upper hand.

Read Widely: Books are your partners in learning. Peruse books on individual budgets, speculations, and personal development to extend your insight.

Take Courses and studios. Sign up for courses or go to studios connected with your field or interests. Deep-rooted acquisition keeps your abilities significant and sharp.

Remain informed. Stay aware of industry patterns, financial turns of events, and emerging advances. Information is power in the financial world.

Look for Guidance: Feel free to seek exhortation and mentorship from the people who have strolled the way to monetary significance before you. Their encounters can be your most noteworthy examples.

Adjust and enhance: Be open to change and advancement. The monetary scene is continually developing, and your capacity to adjust will determine your prosperity.

This fundamental part lays the basis for your journey into monetary significance. By laying out clear objectives, embracing a development mentality, developing discipline, and focusing on consistent learning, you're not simply planning for the road ahead; you're constructing the versatility and assurance necessary to beat difficulties and accomplish your fantasies.

Chapter 2

Monetary Education and Mindset

In the domain of monetary achievement, information genuinely is power. Monetary proficiency is the foundation upon which you'll build your way to thriving. This part plunges profoundly into the significant parts of grasping cash, developing a growing long-term financial stability mentality, and embracing the inescapable dangers that accompany the quest for monetary significance.

Grasping the Essentials of Cash Management

At its center, cash management includes understanding how to carefully deal with your funds. This envelops planning, saving, money management, and overseeing obligations. Begin by making a spending plan that frames your income and costs. This training assists you with following your spending as well as empowering you to apportion assets towards your objectives and needs.

Reserve funds play a basic role in your monetary excursion. Intend to save a piece of your pay reliably, regarding it as a non-debatable cost. This secret stash acts as a security net during unanticipated conditions. Find out about various kinds of speculation, like stocks, securities, common assets, and land. Teach yourself about their dangers and possible returns, empowering you to pursue informed choices.

It is similarly vital to Grasp obligation. Separate between "great" obligations, which might possibly create returns (like understudy loans for instruction), and "awful" obligations, which convey exorbitant interest and offer little worth. Limit superfluous obligations and work on taking care of exorbitant interest obligations as they are fundamentally important.

Developing a Growing Long-Term Financial Stability Mindset

Your considerations and convictions around cash play a critical role in your monetary excursion. Develop a strong financial foundation by moving from a shortage mindset to an overflow mindset. Perceive that there are plentiful open doors for progress and that your endeavors can create huge abundance.

Practice appreciation for what you have while additionally holding nothing back. Encircle yourself with people who share an uplifting outlook on riches and achievement. Participate in certifications and perceptions that support your confidence in your capacity to accomplish monetary significance. Understand that monetary achievement isn't restricted to a limited handful; it's something that anybody can set out upon with the right mentality and procedures.

Embracing Hazard and Gaining from Failure

Monetary development frequently includes venturing into the obscure and going ahead with well-balanced plans of action. Embrace this reality and comprehend that dangers are not really negatives. They are stepping stones to development and advancement. While pursuing informed choices is pivotal, being excessively careful can prompt botched openings.

Expect and acknowledge disappointments as a feature of the excursion. Every disappointment is an illustration that carries you one bit closer to progress. Investigate your disappointments impartially, removing significant bits of knowledge that you can apply to your future undertakings. The capacity to return from misfortunes and use them for your potential benefit is a sign of a versatile and effective person.

Quote: "The best venture you can make is in yourself." Warren Buffett

Warren Buffett's insight typifies the substance of this section. The most significant venture you can make is in your own development and improvement. Training, personal development, and ability-securing are ventures that yield intensifying returns after some time. As you extend your insight and refine your abilities, you improve your ability to make informed choices, jump all over chances, and explore the intricacies of the monetary scene.

Chasing after monetary significance, recall that information enables, attitude impels, and embracing risk speeds up. Furnish yourself with monetary proficiency, cultivate a mentality that invites overflow, and embrace risk as a companion as opposed to an enemy. With these standards as your aide, you're well on your way to becoming amazing at monetary achievement. Remain tuned for the following parts, where we'll investigate the areas of schooling, business, and speculation.

Chapter 3

Instruction and Ability Development

In a rapidly developing world, training and expertise improvement are your compasses, directing you toward the shores of progress. This part dives into the meaning of settling on informed training and vocation decisions, features sought-after fields for what's to come, underlines the benefit of seeking after STEM and tech-related teachers, and highlights the groundbreaking force of web-based learning.

Exploring Training and Profession Choices

Your instructive journey is a significant starting point for your future endeavors. While customary ways, for example, of higher education hold their place, moving toward your schooling with intentionality is fundamental. Ponder your interests, assets, and long-haul objectives. Understand that schooling reaches beyond the study hall; it incorporates independent learning, pragmatic experience, and nonstop development.

Consider the choices accessible: customary universities, professional schools, apprenticeships, and online courses. Every road can furnish you with particular abilities and encounters. Recall that your schooling is a powerful interaction that adjusts to the changing demands of the world.

Popular Fields for the Future

The universe of work is going through a seismic shift. Arising advancements, natural worries, and changes in buyer conduct are reshaping enterprises. To situate yourself for progress, adjust your schooling and abilities to fields that are on the rise.

Fields like computerized reasoning, environmentally friendly power, medical care, online protection, and practical horticulture are projected to encounter huge development. Direct your exploration, converse with experts in these fields, and investigate how your interests meet their requests.

Chasing after STEM and Tech-Related fields

In the computerized age, science, innovation, design, and math (STEM) are the foundations of development. Tech-related fields have become the foundation of enterprises, from medical services to amusement. These disciplines offer assorted open doors for imaginative critical thinking and noteworthy progressions.

Chasing after STEM and tech-related fields not only sets you up for the positions representing things to come but also sharpens your logical reasoning, flexibility, and basic thinking. From programming advancement to information investigation, these abilities have boundless applications that rise above enterprises.

The Force of Online Learning

The computerized insurgency has democratized instruction. Web-based learning stages offer a mother lode of courses, from coding to business across the board, permitting you to fit your schooling to your requirements and timetable. These stages give admission to teachers from around the world, guaranteeing that you learn from the best.

Internet advancement likewise sustains your self-restraint and time-usage abilities. It empowers long-lasting picking up, empowering you to remain refreshed in a speedy world. Furthermore, the capacity to exhibit self-propelled learning is a resource that businesses value.

Quote: "As far as possible, our acknowledgment of tomorrow will be our questions of today." Franklin D. Roosevelt

Franklin D. Roosevelt's words reverberate through the substance of this section. Your true capacity is unlimited, restricted exclusively by your readiness to investigate, learn, and adjust. Training and expertise advancement are your keys to opening entryways of chance and breaking the requirements of uncertainty.

As you explore training and expertise improvement, recall that the world rewards people who are proactive, light-footed, and furnished with the right apparatuses. Furnish yourself with information, embrace change, and saddle yourself with the force of innovation and online assets. Your schooling isn't simply a stepping stone; it's a springboard to your future accomplishments.

In the forthcoming parts, we'll investigate the domains of business, speculation, and systems administration, and that's only the tip of the iceberg, directing you toward an extensive comprehension of the multi-layered excursion to monetary significance.

Chapter 4

Business venture and Innovation

In reality as we know it, where change is the main steady, business ventures and development stand as signals of progress and change. This section investigates the unique scene of business, directing you through the most common way of releasing your imagination, distinguishing potential open doors, and setting out on the excursion of sending off your own business.

Releasing Your Imagination and Creative Spirit

At the core of every business venture lies the capacity to consider new ideas and advance. Innovativeness is the main thrust that powers groundbreaking thoughts, arrangements, and adventures. Embrace your natural imaginative soul and develop a climate that supports advancement.

Look for motivation from different sources, from workmanship and nature to innovation and social patterns. Energize meetings to generate new ideas and coordinated efforts that challenge customary reasoning.

Remember that development frequently comes from clarifying some pressing issues and testing suppositions.

Recognizing Business sector Needs and Opportunities

Enterprising achievement is based on tackling genuine issues and tending to advertise needs. Give close consideration to patterns, buyer conduct, and holes on the lookout. Search for trouble spots that individuals will pay to mitigate. Understand that open doors might emerge from difficulties, changes in innovation, or advancing social elements.

Lead careful statistical surveying to approve your thoughts. Draw in possible clients, accumulate criticism, and refine your ideas in view of their feedback. This iterative cycle guarantees that your business ideas line up with real interest.

Moves toward Sending off Your Own Business

Sending off a business is a thrilling and testing endeavor. It requires cautious preparation, vital execution, and an eagerness to adjust. Separate the cycle into reasonable advances:

1. Conceptualization and Research: Characterize your business thought, ideal interest group, and remarkable

incentive. Research contenders and figure out your industry.

2. Business Plan: Make an extensive, field-tested strategy that frames your objectives, methodologies, monetary projections, and showcasing approaches.

3. Legal and Monetary Setup: Register your business, get essential licenses, and set up a monetary structure. Look for proficient exhortation to guarantee consistency with legitimate and burdensome necessities.

4. Building Your Item or Service: Foster your item or service by guaranteeing quality and addressing client needs.

5. Marketing and Branding: Creating a convincing brand character and promoting techniques Influence the advanced stages to successfully arrive at your interest group.

6. Launch and Feedback: Send off your business and accumulate criticism from starting clients. Utilize this input to make important enhancements.

7. Scaling and Growth: As your business builds momentum, center around scaling activities, extending your client base, and investigating new roads for development.

Quote: "As far as possible, our acknowledgment of tomorrow will be our questions of today." Franklin D. Roosevelt

Franklin D. Roosevelt's statement typifies the essence of business and advancement. Questions and fears can impede progress, yet beating them prompts unlimited conceivable outcomes. Put stock in your capability to make change and have a constructive outcome.

As you leave on your enterprising excursion, remember that development is energized by interest, critical thinking, and an eagerness to learn from disappointments. Each step you take is a move to learn, adjust, and inch closer to progress. Remain receptive, tough, and focused on the master plan for building something significant.

In the impending sections, we'll dive into the domains of speculation, systems administration, wellbeing, and offset, furnishing you with a thorough tool stash for your journey to financial significance.

Chapter 5

Venture and Abundance Creation

Speculation is the specialty of sowing seeds today to procure a plentiful harvest from here on out. This part digs into the fundamental parts of speculation and abundance creation, directing you through understanding different venture vehicles, practicing expansion and chance administration, building automated sources of income, and investigating the domains of land and financial exchange ventures.

Grasping Different Venture Vehicles

Speculation and valuable open doors are pretty much as different as the objectives they serve. From stocks and bonds to land and new companies, every venture vehicle has its own gamble and brings profile back. It's essential to grasp these choices and adjust them to your monetary targets and hazard resilience.

1. Stocks and Equities: Putting resources into public corporations offers the potential for capital appreciation. Stocks are known for their liquidity and potential for

significant yields, yet they likewise accompany higher instability.

2. Bonds: Bonds are fixed-pay protections given by legislatures or enterprises. They offer ordinary interest installments and are, for the most part, considered lower-risk than stocks.

3. Mutual Assets and ETFs: These subsidizes pool cash from different financial backers to put resources into a broadened arrangement of resources. They give admission to various ventures with differing levels of chance.

4. Real Estate: Land speculation incorporates private and business properties. Land can produce rental pay and value over the long haul, offering both pay and possible capital increases.

5. Startups and Confidential Equity: Putting resources into new businesses and privately owned businesses offers high-risk, high-reward potential. It requires a cautiously expected level of effort and is frequently appropriate for experienced financial backers.

Broadening and Hazard Management

The well-established aphorism "don't tie up your resources in one place" sounds valid in the realm of financial planning. Expansion includes spreading your ventures across various resource classes to decrease risk. A differentiated portfolio can assist in relieving the effects of a decline in a specific area.

Also, risk the board is essential. Comprehend the gamble related to every speculation and survey whether it lines up with your gamble resilience. Consider your speculation skyline and monetary objectives while deciding.

Building Automated revenue streams

Automated revenue is the sacred goal of abundance creation. It's pay acquired with insignificant continuous exertion or dynamic contribution. Building automated sources of income permits you to break free from the ideal opportunity for cash trade and achieve monetary autonomy.

Recurring, automated revenue sources can incorporate investment properties, profit-paying stocks, eminences from imaginative works, and pay produced by online organizations. The key is to contribute time, exertion, and assets forthrightly to make economical revenue streams that work for you over the long haul.

Investigating Land and Financial exchange Investments

Land and the financial exchange are two of the most notable speculation roads, each with one-of-a-kind qualities.

1. Real Estate: Putting resources into land includes buying properties for rental income or capital appreciation. Land can provide a constant flow of recurring, automated revenue and possibly value over the long run. Research the market, area, and potential for rental interest prior to effective financial planning.

2. Stock Market: Putting resources into public corporations through stocks offers the potential for long-term capital development. Nonetheless, the financial exchange can be unstable, so a drawn-out viewpoint is significant. Consider expanding your stock across various businesses and areas.

As you set out on the journey of venture and abundance creation, remember that information is your most noteworthy resource. Teach yourself about various speculation choices, foster an unmistakable procedure, and look for proficient guidance when required. Speculation is a drawn-out endeavor, and by pursuing informed choices and remaining restrained, you can bridle the force of compounding and accomplish your monetary objectives.

In the impending sections, we'll investigate the domains of systems administration, wellbeing, health, and balance between fun and serious activities, giving you a balanced manual for accomplishing monetary significance.

Chapter 6

Systems administration and Relationship Building

In the embroidery of progress, the strings of systems administration and relationship building weave a texture of chances and associations. This section digs into the significant meaning of developing areas of strength, tackling the force of virtual entertainment and online stages, looking for mentorship, and gathering shrewdness from accomplished people.

The Significance of Building Serious areas of strength

Your organization is a supply of conceivable outcomes. Each association you make, each relationship you support, holds the possibility to open entryways and prepare for coordinated effort, development, and more development. Building serious areas of strength for an organization isn't just about gathering people to get in touch with; it's tied in with encouraging certified connections in light of trust, regard, and shared interests.

Encircling yourself with a different gathering of people—guides, companions, partners, and companions—establishes a climate where thoughts thrive and valuable open doors arise. Your organization can share experiences, make suggestions, and even acquaint you with expected financial backers, accomplices, or clients.

Utilizing Virtual Entertainment and Online platforms

The advanced age has reclassified organizing, making it conceivable to interface with individuals across the globe from the solace of your own space. Web-based entertainment and online stages are your virtual stages, where you can showcase your skills, share significant bits of knowledge, and draw in a larger crowd.

Pick stages that line up with your objectives and interests. LinkedIn, for example, is an incredible asset for proficient systems administration, while platforms like X and Instagram can assist you with laying out your own image. Share content that adds esteem, sparks discussions, and exhibits your unique point of view.

Mentorship and Gaining from Effective Individuals

Mentorship is a compass that guides you through strange domains. Learning from people who have strolled the way you seek to cross can speed up your development and provide significant illustrations from their encounters. Search out coaches whose qualities and accomplishments impact you.

A coach can give direction, offer criticism, and challenge your suspicions. Their bits of knowledge can assist you in exploring difficulties, making informed choices, and staying away from normal traps. Recall that mentorship is a two-way street; contribute your excitement, commitment, and readiness to learn accordingly.

Quote: "Your organization is your total assets." Watchman Gale

Watchman Hurricane's concise statement embodies the essence of this section. The associations you develop are not simply numbers; they are the money of chances. Your organization extends your points of view, acquaints you with new points of view, and opens entryways that could some way or another stay shut.

As you construct connections, remember that validity and correspondence are vital. Offer your help and abilities to others, however much you look for them for yourself. Develop significant associations, sustain them with care, and watch how they enhance your journey toward monetary greatness.

OuxIn the impending parts, we'll investigate the domains of wellbeing, health, balance between serious and fun activities, offering in return, and social effect, giving you an all-encompassing way to deal with making a daily existence that is both prosperous and satisfying.

Chapter 7

Wellbeing, Health, and Balance between fun and serious activities

Chasing after monetary significance, it's memorable and fundamental that genuine flourishing envelops something other than material riches. This part dives into the principal significance of focusing on your physical and mental prosperity, accomplishing an amicable balance between serious and fun activities, and embracing methodologies to oversee pressure and forestall burnout.

Focusing on Physical and Psychological wellness

Your body and brain are the establishments whereupon you construct your fantasies. Ignoring your wellbeing can make you think twice about your capacity to partake in your rewards for so much hard work. Focus on normal activity, adjusted nourishment, and adequate rest. These practices improve your actual imperativeness as well as your mental capacities and versatility.

Similarly significant is your psychological wellness. Practice care, reflection, or journaling to develop close-to-home prosperity. Look for proficient assistance when required; recognizing and tending to emotional well-being difficulties is an indication of solidarity, not shortcoming.

achieving Balance between serious and fun activities for long-haul Achievement

While desire drives you forward, keeping a balance between serious and fun activities is essential for supporting achievement. Finding some kind of harmony is a craft that requires cognizant exertion. Assign time for work, yet additionally account for relaxation, family, companions, and special goals.

Perceive that your adequacy at work is intently attached to your prosperity. Burnout can destroy your efficiency and inventiveness. Put down stopping points and honor them. Lay out a reasonable deadline for work and focus on turning it off during your relaxation hours.

Procedures for Overseeing Pressure and Burnout

Stress is a characteristic piece of the excursion, but overseeing it really is urgent. Distinguish stressors and foster ways of dealing with especially difficult times. Normal activity, reflection, profound breathing, and taking part in side interests can assist with mitigating pressure.

Burnout, then again, is a persistent condition of physical and close-to-home fatigue that comes about because of drawn-out pressure. To forestall burnout, practice taking care of oneself, enjoy reprieves, and focus on exercises that give you pleasure. Recall that you can't pour from a vacant cup; dealing with yourself is essential for dealing with your desires.

Quote: "There's no need to focus on having time; it's tied in with setting aside a few minutes." Sixtus John

This statement fills in as a strong update that time is an asset you have the organization to distribute. It underscores the need to intentionally focus on what makes a difference in your well-being, connections, and prosperity. Setting aside a few minutes for exercises that re-energize you shows interest in your drawn-out progress and joy.

As you explore the convergences of wellbeing, health, and balance between fun and serious activities, recall that these angles are not isolated from your quest for monetary significance; they are indispensable to it. At the point when your body and psyche are one, your capacity to quickly jump all over chances, use wise judgment, and partake in the rewards of your endeavors enhances. The impending parts will investigate the features of offering in return, social effect, and passing on an enduring heritage, a demonstration of the all-encompassing methodology you're embracing on your journey.

Chapter 8

Offering in return and Social Impact

As you climb the stepping stool of progress, remember that the proportion of your significance lies in what you accomplish for yourself as well as in the positive effect you have on other people. This part dives into the significant delight of charity and giving, the groundbreaking capability of making social change through business, and the heritage-building effect of liberality.

The Delight of Charity and Giving

Magnanimity is the specialty of sharing your assets to elevate and work on the existences of others. It's an update that, as you succeed, you have the ability to have a significant effect on the planet. Taking part in humanitarian endeavors benefits others, sustains your spirit, and improves your sense of direction.

Whether you contribute monetarily, volunteer your time, or utilize your foundation to bring issues to light, charity connects you to a larger local area and intensifies your positive impact. Recall that giving doesn't need to be fabulous; even little thoughtful gestures can have a significant effect.

Making Positive Social Change Through business

Business can be a strong impetus for social change. Embrace the idea of cognizant free enterprise, where your strategic approaches line up with values like manageability, social obligation, and a moral way of behaving. Consider how your items or administration can contribute to settling cultural difficulties.

Organizations that focus on friendly effects frequently partake in serious areas of strength such as standing, representative commitment, and client unwaveringly. By incorporating reason into your plan of action, you can gradually expand influence that goes a long way beyond monetary exchanges.

Building a Tradition of Effect and Generosity

Your inheritance is the story you abandon a story that reaches out past your lifetime. While monetary achievement is an eminent accomplishment, it's your effect on individuals' lives and the world that genuinely characterizes your heritage. Consider the causes you're energetic about and the sort of effect you need to make.

Liberality is a heritage-building resource. Through generosity, mentorship, and sharing your insight, you plant seeds of positive change that keep on developing long after you're gone. Recollect that your activities have the ability to motivate others to contribute to a superior world.

Quote: "We earn enough to pay the rent by what we get; however, we make a daily existence by what we give." Winston Churchill

Winston Churchill's statement embodies the substance of this section. While monetary achievement empowers you to get by, the demonstration of giving enhances your life. Through giving, you create a legacy that resounds a long way past material accomplishments, making a permanent imprint on the existence of those you contact.

As you embrace the ideas of offering in return and social effect, recall that your excursion to monetary significance acquires much more importance when it's entwined with the prosperity of others. The forthcoming parts will give a reflection on your surprising excursion and experiences in embracing your future with great affection, an abundance of information, and a heart brimming with reason.

Conclusion

As you come to the end of this book, you stand at the intersection of your journey, an excursion that rises above monetary achievement and wanders into the domain of importance. You've left in a way that consolidates desire with reason, winding around together information, outlook, activity, and effect. Your journey to monetary greatness isn't just a quest for riches; a journey shapes your personality, impacts your decisions, and contacts the existence of people around you.

You've found the force of beginning youthful, perceiving that each choice you make today reverberates into your future. The sections have directed you through the complexities of monetary proficiency, training, business ventures, speculation, organizing, wellbeing, health, the balance between fun and serious activities, and the groundbreaking effect of offering in return. Every feature of this excursion is a string that meshes into the texture of your life, making an embroidery of accomplishment and reason.

Recall that significance isn't characterized exclusively by the zeros in your ledger, but rather by the lives you contact, the thoughts you rouse, and the changes you make. As you move forward, keep on embracing the insights shared in these pages:

Enable Your Mindset: Develop strength, imagination, and a development outlook. Your convictions shape your existence, and your demeanor decides your height.

Influence Your Network: Your organization is a wellspring of undiscovered capacity. Support connections, look for mentorship, and team up with others to intensify your effect.

Focus on Well-Being: Your prosperity is its underpinning. Focus on your physical, mental, and close-to-home wellbeing and maintain a reasonable work-life balance.

Embrace Innovation: Business ventures and development are the engines of progress. Embrace change, go ahead with carefully thought-out plans of action, and let your imagination thrive.

Put resources into Your future: Vital speculation is the way to abundance and creation. Differentiate your portfolio, look for open doors, and develop recurring sources of income.

Offer in return and Leave a legacy: The delight of giving and the force of effect are your heritage. Add to positive change, elevate others, and make an enduring blemish on the world.

Your excursion from progress to importance is a nonstop development of an ensemble made out of your accomplishments, learnings, and commitments. As you explore the way to monetary significance, recollect that each step is a demonstration of your true capacity, your flexibility, and your obligation to make a day-to-day existence that is both prosperous and significant.

What's to come unfurls before you, a material anticipating your brushstrokes. Embrace it with fortitude, embrace it with interest, and embrace it with the unflinching conviction that you have the ability to shape your predetermination. Your journey to monetary achievement isn't simply an objective; it's a long-lasting experience, an excursion that will keep on unfolding with every decision you make, each move you initiate, and every heart you contact.

Embrace the way before you, for the actual excursion holds the substance of your significance. May your journey be overflowing with bliss, reason, and the acknowledgment of your most elevated potential. Here's to your journey, may it be sweet, lovely, and remarkably your own.

Appendix

This appendix is your toolkit, an invaluable resource to supplement your journey to financial greatness. It offers a curated selection of recommended books, podcasts, and resources to deepen your understanding, sample investment portfolios tailored to different stages of life, and actionable steps to kickstart your journey and put the principles discussed in this book into practice.

Recommended Books, Podcasts, and Resources

Books:
1. "Rich Dad Poor Dad" by Robert Kiyosaki
2. "The Millionaire Next Door" by Thomas J. Stanley and William D. Danko
3. "The Intelligent Investor" by Benjamin Graham
4. "You Are a Badass at Making Money" by Jen Sincero
5. "The Compound Effect" by Darren Hardy

Podcasts:
1. "The Tim Ferriss Show" - Tim Ferriss
2. "The BiggerPockets Money Podcast" - Mindy Jensen and Scott Trench
3. "The Tony Robbins Podcast" - Tony Robbins
4. "The InvestED Podcast" - Phil Town and Danielle Town
5. "The School of Greatness" - Lewis Howes

Online Resources:
1. Investopedia (www.investopedia.com)
2. BiggerPockets (www.biggerpockets.com)
3. Coursera (www.coursera.org)
4. Khan Academy (www.khanacademy.org)
5. TED Talks (www.ted.com)

Sample Investment Portfolios for Different Stages

Early Career:
- 70% in a diversified stock market index fund
- 20% in a bond fund for stability
- 10% in a small allocation of high-risk, high-reward investments (e.g., individual stocks, cryptocurrencies)

Mid-Career:
- 60% in diversified stock funds
- 20% in bonds
- 10% in real estate investment trusts (REITs)
- 10% in individual stocks or a mix of other investments

Approaching Retirement:
- 40% in diversified stock funds
- 30% in bonds
- 15% in dividend-paying stocks
- 10% in alternative investments (e.g., peer-to-peer lending, commodities)
- 5% in cash or cash equivalents

Actionable Steps to Kickstart Your Journey

1.   Set Clear Goals: Define your short-term and long-term financial goals. Make them specific, measurable, achievable, relevant, and time-bound (SMART).

2.   Educate Yourself: invest time in learning about financial literacy, investing, and personal finance. Read books, take online courses, and follow reputable financial experts.

3.   Create a Budget: Establish a budget that tracks your income and expenses. Allocate funds for saving, investing, and achieving your financial goals.

4.   Start Investing Early: Begin investing as soon as possible. Take advantage of compounding to maximize the growth of your investments over time.

5.   Build a Network: Actively seek out networking opportunities. Attend seminars, workshops, and industry events to connect with like-minded individuals.

6.   Prioritize Health and Well-Being: Incorporate regular exercise, balanced nutrition, and stress-relief practices into your routine. Maintain a healthy work-life balance.

7.   Explore Entrepreneurship: If you're inclined, consider starting business that aligns with your passions and skills. Focus on adding value to your customers and solving real problems.

8. Give Back: Dedicate time or resources to philanthropic efforts. Whether it's volunteering or contributing to causes you're passionate about, your impact matters.

9. Seek Mentorship: Identify potential mentors who can guide you in your personal and professional growth. Learn from their experiences and insights.

10. Review and Adjust: Regularly review your financial plan, investment portfolio, and goals. Be open to adjusting your strategies based on changing circumstances.

Your journey to financial greatness is an ongoing endeavor that requires dedication, education, and action. The principles discussed in this book are your compass, and the resources provided in this appendix are your tools. As you progress, remember that each step you take, no matter how small, brings you closer to achieving your aspirations. Embrace the journey, seize opportunities, and continue to craft a life that is both prosperous and fulfilling.

Put forth Clear Objectives and adopt a Development Mentality that fits Your journey.

Putting forth clear objectives and developing a development mentality are two primary points of support that support your excursion to monetary significance. These components provide guidance and the psychological structure necessary to explore the difficulties and potential open doors that lie ahead.

Setting Clear goals

Imagine setting out on an excursion without an objective as a main priority. Objectives provide your excursion's motivation and course. To set out on your way to monetary significance, setting clear, distinct goals is fundamental. How it's done:

1. Be Specific: Characterize your objectives in exact terms. For example, to accomplish monetary autonomy, indicate how much cash you really want to have and the timetable within which you intend to accomplish it.

2. Make Them measurable: Evaluate your objectives so you can keep tabs on your development. Unmistakable measurements assist you in evaluating your accomplishments and remaining motivated.

3. Ensure They're Achievable: While aspiration is exemplary, laying out unreachable objectives can

prompt disappointment. Guarantee that your objectives are practical given your ongoing conditions and assets.

4. Relevance Matters: Your objectives ought to align with your qualities and yearnings. They ought to be significant and important to you, driving your assurance to accomplish them.

5. Set Time Frames: Lay out cutoff times for your objectives. Having a period-bound target makes you want to get a move on and assists you with arranging your activities in a similar manner.

Taking on a Development Mindset

A development mentality is the conviction that your capacities and knowledge can be created through exertion, learning, and tirelessness. Comprehending difficulties and misfortunes are open doors for development, not signs of deficiency. This is the way to develop a development mentality:

1. Embrace Challenges: View difficulties as stepping stones to progress. Rather than avoiding troubles, move toward them as opportunities to acquire and foster new abilities.

2. View exercise as a Way to Mastery: Understand that achievement requires difficult work and predictable exertion. The more you put resources into, learning and practicing, the better your results will be.

3. Learn from setbacks: Instead of deciphering disappointment as a last decision, treat it as an important example. Break down what turned out badly, adjust your methodology, and utilize the experience for your potential benefit.

4. Seek Feedback: Useful analysis gives experiences to progress. Welcome criticism from tutors, friends, or associates, and use it to refine your techniques.

5. Be Motivated by Others' succes: As opposed to feeling compromised by others' accomplishments, let them rouse you. Perceive that their achievements are a demonstration of what's conceivable through commitment and exertion.

6. Persist Even with Adversity: A development outlook empowers flexibility. When confronted with difficulties, keep up your assurance and stay focused on your objectives.

By defining clear objectives and adopting a journey. Objectives keep you centered, giving you an objective to endeavor toward, while a development outlook furnishes you with the mentality necessary to defeat snags and consistently advance.

Keep in mind that your objectives are yet to be determined; they can adjust as conditions change. Moreover, a development mentality is a muscle you can reinforce over the long haul. As you progress along your way to monetary significance, these components will act as your directing lights, enlightening the way forward and engaging you to accomplish your fantasies.

Explore the Changing Scene of Instruction and Vocation Choices

In a time of quick mechanical advances and moving enterprises, the scene of schooling and profession decisions is dynamic and steadily advancing. Exploring this scene requires a mix of foreknowledge, flexibility, and an essential way to deal with building your range of abilities. This is the way you can really diagram your course through this groundbreaking excursion:

1. Consider Your Interests and Strengths:
Start by introspecting and recognizing your interests, assets, and hobbies. What subjects or exercises impact you? What abilities easily fall into place for you? Adjusting your schooling and vocation decisions to your inborn capacities can lay a strong foundation for your excursion.

2. Remain Informed about emerging Trends:
Remain inquisitive and informed. Keep a pulse on emerging patterns, mechanical headways, and changes in the gig market. What businesses are developing? What abilities are popular? Being proactive in looking for this data positions you to make informed choices.

3. Embrace deep-rooted learning:
In the present high-speed world, learning is a deep-rooted endeavor. Conventional instruction is only one piece of the puzzle. Seek constant learning through web-based courses, studios, and workshops. This upgrades your range of abilities as well as exhibiting your versatility to likely bosses.

4. Consider Modern Paths:
Perceive that conventional professional education is, by all accounts, not the only way to progress. Professional schools, apprenticeships, and online affirmations offer elective courses that can prompt compensating vocations. Assess your choices and pick the one that best fits your objectives.

5. Adjust to Ability Demand:
Businesses advance, as do the abilities they require. Turn and secure new abilities that are pertinent to the present employment market. Abilities like coding, information examination, and computerized advertising have colossal applications and are pursued in different enterprises.

6. Systems administration and Industry insights:
Organizing is important while exploring the instruction and vocation scene. Go to industry

occasions, courses, and studios to interface with experts who can give experiences into the requests of their fields. This firsthand data can direct your decisions.

7. Look for Mentorship:
Tutors can give priceless direction in light of their own encounters. Look for coaches inside your ideal industry or vocation way. Their bits of knowledge can assist you with keeping away from normal traps and pursue informed choices.

8. Grow Delicate skills:
Specialized abilities are fundamental, but delicate abilities are similarly significant. Correspondence, critical thinking, flexibility, and cooperation are characteristics that businesses esteem. Develop these abilities to hang out in a cutthroat work market.

9. Versatility is Key:
The capacity to adjust is a sign of progress in this evolving scene. Be ready for changes in your chosen field and be available to investigate new headings if necessary. Embracing change can open surprising doors.

10. Seek after What Lines up with Your values.

Your schooling and profession decisions ought to line up with your qualities and yearnings. Consider the effect you need to make, the work culture that suits you, and the way of life you imagine. A feeling of direction will fuel your obligation to go your way.

Exploring the training and vocation scene requires an equilibrium between practicality and enthusiasm. Embrace change, quickly jump all over chances, and move toward each step with an eagerness to learn and develop. By remaining receptive to arising patterns, leveling up your abilities, and encouraging significant associations, you can proactively shape your schooling and profession venture toward a fate of vastly conceivable outcomes.

Embrace Business venture and Development as Apparatuses for Abundance creation.

Business venture and development are twin motors that drive progress, flash monetary development, and make roads for people to accomplish monetary significance. In a quickly impacting world, the capacity to develop and proceed with carefully thought out plans of action through business venture has become more imperative than any other time. This is the way you can outfit these useful assets for abundance creation:

1. Develop a Culture of Imagination:
Advancement originates from imagination. Support a mentality that values imaginative reasoning, critical thinking, and investigating eccentric thoughts. Cultivate a climate where it are invited to conceptualize and share inventive arrangements.

2. Recognize Market Holes and needs:
Effective business people distinguish between holes on the lookout and requirements that are neglected or underserved. Notice patterns, pay attention to client input, and study emerging advancements to uncover open doors for development.

3. Embrace Hazard and Disappointment:
A business venture implies determined risk-taking. Understand that disappointment isn't the end, but a stepping stone to progress. Gain from your

disappointments, emphasize your thoughts, and adjust your methodologies in view of the illustrations you learn.

4. Foster an Interesting Incentive:
In a cutthroat scene, a remarkable offer separates you. Obviously, describe what separates your item or administration from the rest. How can it tackle an issue or upgrade the existence of your main interest group?

5. Test and approve your thoughts:
Prior to sending off on a full-scale adventure, test your thoughts on a smaller scale. Make models, lead reviews, and accumulate criticism from expected clients. This limits the gamble of putting resources into a thought that may not resonate with the market.

6. Influence Innovation and Advanced stages:
The computerized age offers extraordinary opportunities for business visionaries. Influence innovation to smooth out tasks, contact a worldwide crowd, and make versatile arrangements. Internet business, virtual entertainment, and web-based showcasing are useful assets available to you.

7. Fabricate Areas of strength for:
Organizing is fundamental for business visionaries. Encircle yourself with coaches, counselors, and similar people who can offer direction and backing. Systems administration can open doors to associations, financing, and significant bits of knowledge.

8. Gain from Client criticism:
Client criticism is an important asset for refining your contributions. Stand by listening to your clients, adjust to their inclinations, and ceaselessly work on your items or administrations in view of their feedback.

9. Look for Financing admirably:
While business ventures frequently require capital, look for financing carefully. Investigate different choices, for example, bootstrapping, private supporters, funding, or crowdfunding. Comprehend the terms and ramifications of each subsidizing source.

10. Scale with Purpose:
As your endeavor builds up some decent forward momentum, center around reasonable development. Keep harmony among development and keep up with the nature of your contributions. Scaling too quickly without a legitimate framework can prompt failure.

11. Embrace Social and Natural effects:
Development can stretch past past benefits to have a social and natural effect. Consider how your business can contribute emphatically to society while making money. Embrace reasonable practices and social obligations.

12. Endure with Passion:
Business is an adventure of ups and downs. Constancy is critical. Energy for your thoughts and a solid feeling of direction will keep you propelled during testing times.

By embracing business ventures and advancement, you tap into the force of making respect, tackling issues, and molding enterprises. Whether you're beginning a private venture, sending off a tech startup, or upsetting a current field, your capacity to improve and rejuvenate novel thoughts can prompt both monetary achievement and an enduring effect on the world. Through innovativeness, a carefully thought-out plan of action, and a steady obligation to greatness, you can bridle these devices to clear your way to abundance creation and then some.

Foster a Profound Comprehension of Monetary Education and Cash management among executives.

Monetary proficiency is the foundation of your excursion into monetary significance. It's the information and abilities you really want to come to educated and successful conclusions about your funds. From planning to money management, having serious areas of strength in monetary education enables you to assume command over your monetary predetermination. This is the way to foster this vital range of abilities:

1. Ace the Fundamentals:
Start with the basics. Comprehend key ideas like planning, saving, obligation to the board, and accumulating funds. These essentials give a strong foundation to your monetary excursion.

2. Make a Spending plan:
A spending plan is your monetary guide. Track your pay and costs, allotting assets to necessities, reserve funds, ventures, and optional spending. A very organized spending plan guarantees your cash is aligned with your objectives.

3. Oversee Obligation Astutely:

Not all obligations are terrible; however, it is pivotal to oversee them. Separate between great obligation (like interests in training or land) and terrible obligation (exorbitant interest charge card obligation). Intend to take care of exorbitant interest obligations first.

4. Construct a Rainy day account:
Life is eccentric, and having a backup stash gives you a security net. Plan to save three to a half year's worth of everyday costs in a fluid account to cover unexpected circumstances.

5. Figure out Venture Vehicles:
Teach yourself about different speculation choices—stocks, securities, common assets, land—and that's just the beginning. Enhance your portfolio to oversee risk and possibly acquire better yields.

6. Embrace and build interest:
Building interest is an amazing asset for abundance creation. It's the compounding phenomenon, where your cash develops on your underlying venture as well as on the premium it acquires after some time.

7. Put forth Monetary objectives:

Objectives provide motivation for your monetary excursion. Put forth momentary objectives (e.g., taking care of a Mastercard) and long-haul objectives (e.g., retirement arranging). Objectives assist you in remaining on track and measuring progress.

8. Put resources into Your Schooling:
Similarly, as you put resources into monetary resources, put resources into your monetary schooling. Understand books, take courses, go to workshops, and remain refreshed on financial patterns and market advancements.

9. Plan for Retirement:
Begin anticipating retirement early. Add to retirement accounts like 401(k)s or IRAs to exploit tax reductions and guarantee an agreeable retirement.

10. Safeguard Yourself:
Protection is a type of monetary security. Think about medical coverage, disaster protection, and property protection to defend yourself and your resources from startling occasions.

11. Look for Proficient Guidance:

If necessary, consult monetary consultants, organizers, or bookkeepers. Their ability can assist you in making informed choices aligned with your objectives.

12. Show Monetary Proficiency to Other people:
Share your insight with loved ones. Advancing monetary education locally engages others to assume command over their monetary fates.

Monetary proficiency is definitely not a one-time try; it's a continuous obligation to persistent learning and improvement. As you imagine how you might interpret cash on the board, you're constructing a strong starting point for monetary achievement. With each step you take, you're upgrading your capacity to use wise judgment, expand potential open doors, and make a daily existence that is both monetarily secure and satisfying.

Fabricate an Organization of Tutors and Similar people.

On the excursion to monetary significance, your organization is in excess of an assortment of reaches; it's a unique biological system of help, direction, and motivation. Encircling yourself with coaches and similar people upgrades your own and proficient development, extends your viewpoints, and opens ways to potential open doors you probably won't have envisioned. This is the way to fabricate an organization that pushes you forward:

1. Distinguish Your Objectives:
Explain your objectives and goals. What regions would you like to succeed in? What businesses would you say you are keen on? Having a reasonable internal compass will direct you in picking coaches and associations that line up with your excursion.

2. Look for Mentorship:
Tutors are capable people who can offer bits of knowledge, exhortation, and direction in view of their own encounters. Search for tutors who have accomplished what you try to accomplish and who share your qualities.

3. Show Certifiable Interest:
Move toward expected guides and associations with real interest. Express your deference for their accomplishments and make sense of why you esteem

their ability. Validness is critical to building significant connections.

4. Be Available to input:
Guides are important wellsprings of input. Be open to their direction and useful analysis. Their bits of knowledge can assist you with distinguishing vulnerable sides and work on your procedures.

5. Offer Worth in Return:
Mentorship is a two-way road. While you gain from their insight, give esteem as a trade off. Fabricate an Organization of Tutors and Similar people.

On the excursion to monetary significance, your organization is in excess of an assortment of reaches; it's a unique biological system of help, direction, and motivation. Encircling yourself with tutors and similar people improves your own and proficient development, extends your points of view, and opens ways to amazing open doors you probably won't have envisioned. This is the way to fabricate an organization that drives you forward:

1. Distinguish Your Objectives:
Explain your objectives and goals. What regions would you like to succeed in? What businesses would you say you are keen on? Having a reasonable internal compass will direct you in picking guides and associations that line up with your excursion.

2. Look for Mentorship:

Tutors are capable people who can offer bits of knowledge, exhortation, and direction in light of their own encounters. Search for coaches who have accomplished what you try to accomplish and who share your qualities.

3. Show Real Interest:

Move toward possible tutors and associations with certifiable interest. Express your reverence for their accomplishments and make sense of why you esteem their skill. Realness is critical to building significant connections.

4. Be Available to input:

Coaches are important wellsprings of criticism. Be responsive to their direction and helpful analysis. Their experiences can assist you with recognizing vulnerable sides and work on your systems.

5. Offer Worth in Return:

Mentorship is a two-way road. While you gain from their insight, give esteem as a trade off. This could be through sharing your extraordinary viewpoints, helping with their tasks, or contributing your abilities.

6. Go to Systems administration occasions:

Industry occasions, gatherings, and classes give fantastic chances to meet similar people and expected tutors. Participate in discussions, trade contact data, and follow up a short time later.

7. Join Online people group:
Virtual stages, for example, LinkedIn gatherings, online discussions, and web-based entertainment networks, empower you to associate with experts from around the world who share your inclinations.

8. Participate in Cooperative Ventures:
Cooperative tasks or adventures can areas of strength for manufacture. Cooperating on a shared objective upgrades your abilities as well as encourages trust and fellowship.

9. Influence Web-based Entertainment:
Web-based entertainment stages furnish a way to associate with people you probably won't have the chance to meet face to face. Understand thought pioneers, take part in conversations, and fabricate connections on the web.

10. Go to Studios and classes:
Partake in studios and workshops drove by specialists in your field. These occasions offer significant systems administration potential open doors and experiences from achieved people.

11. Be Proactive in Offering in return:
Show proactive kindness by tutoring others as you progress. Sharing your insights and encounters helps other people, grows your organization, and cements your own comprehension.

12. Keep up with Relationships:
Organizing isn't just about making associations; it's tied in with supporting them. Keep in contact with your coaches and associations, updating them on your progress and looking for their recommendations when required.

Keep in mind that your organization is an impression of your desires and values. The connections you develop have the ability to shape your excursion. Through mentorship and associations, you're acquiring bits of knowledge with monetary significance, but at the same time, you're adding to a local area of shared learning and development. As you construct your organization, embrace the open door to both get and give, and watch how these connections lead you to success. This could be through sharing your interesting points of view, helping with their activities, or contributing your abilities.

6. Go to Systems Administration occasions:
Industry occasions, gatherings, and courses give phenomenal chances to meet similar people and possible coaches. Participate in discussions, trade contact data, and follow up a short time later.

7. Join an online group:
Virtual stages, for example, LinkedIn gatherings, online discussions, and web-based entertainment networks, empower you to associate with experts from around the world who share your inclinations.

8. Participate in Cooperative Undertakings:
Cooperative tasks or adventures can be serious areas of strength for fashion. Cooperating on a shared objective upgrades your abilities as well as cultivates trust and brotherhood.

9. Influence Virtual Entertainment:
Virtual entertainment stages furnish a way to interface with people you probably won't have the chance to meet face-to-face. Understand thought pioneers, participate in conversations, and assemble connections on the web.

10. Go to Studios and courses:
Partake in studios and courses led by specialists in your field. These occasions offer significant system administration open doors and experiences from accomplished people.

11. Be Proactive in Offering in return:
Show proactive kindness by coaching others as you progress. Sharing your insights and encounters helps other people, grows your organization, and hardens your own comprehension.

12. Keep up with Relationships:
Organizing isn't just about making associations; it's also about sustaining them. Keep in contact with your tutors and associations, updating them on your progress and looking for their recommendations when required.

Keep in mind that your organization is an impression of your desires and values. The connections you develop have the ability to shape your excursion. Through mentorship and associations, you're acquiring bits of knowledge with monetary significance, but on the other hand, you're adding to a local area of shared learning and development. As you fabricate your organization, embrace the open door to both get and give, and watch how *these connections lift you to progress.*

Focus on well-being, Health, and a balance between fun and serious activities for Supported achievement.

Chasing after monetary significance, your most prominent resource isn't your financial balance; it's your physical and mental prosperity. Focusing on wellbeing and health and accomplishing an agreeable balance between serious and fun activities are not simply discretionary extravagances; they're fundamental parts that fuel your excursion toward enduring achievement. This is the way to guarantee your prosperity stays at the very front:

1. Perceive the Significance of Taking care of oneself:
Taking care of oneself isn't self-centered; it's an interest in your capacity to perform at your best. Focus on exercises that revive your body and psyche, whether it's activity, reflection, perusing, or investing energy with friends and family.

2. Keep a Reasonable Way of Life:
Make progress toward balance in all parts of your life. Designate time not exclusively to your work but additionally to side interests, connections,

self-awareness, and relaxation exercises that give you pleasure.

3. Set Clear Boundaries:
Limits are vital for maintaining a balance between fun and serious activities. Lay out set working hours and fight the temptation to browse messages or business-related assignments during your own time.

4. Integrate Customary activity:
Actual work is the foundation of wellbeing. Normal activity helps your actual wellbeing as well as improves your psychological clarity and decreases pressure.

5. Focus on Nourishment and hydration:
Good dieting and remaining hydrated fuel your body and brain. Consume a healthy eating routine rich in supplements and keep up with satisfactory hydration to support your energy levels.

6. Practice Care and Stress decrease:
Care methods like reflection, profound breathing, and yoga can assist you with managing pressure and improve your psychological prosperity. These practices advance a feeling of quiet and concentration.

7. Get Quality rest.
Rest is fundamental for mental capability, temperament guidelines, and general wellbeing. Focus on getting sufficient, soothing rest every night to help your physical and mental imperativeness.

8. Disengage from Innovation:
Steady availability can prompt burnout. Commit time every day to separate from screens and participate in exercises that don't include innovation.

9. Enjoy Customary reprieves:
Stay balanced by integrating customary breaks into your working day. Brief breaks further develop efficiency, inventiveness, and, generally speaking, mental prosperity.

10. Take part in recreational exercises:
Side interests and recreation exercises give a truly necessary outlet for unwinding and delight. Whether it's perusing, painting, or playing an instrument, these exercises improve your life.

11. Encourage Significant Connections:

Solid connections add to your close-to-home prosperity. Invest quality energy with loved ones who offer help and a feeling of association.

12. Embrace Adaptability:
Adaptability is fundamental to maintaining a balance between serious and fun activities. Embrace remote work choices, adaptable timetables, and the capacity to adjust to evolving conditions.

Focusing on wellbeing, health, and a balance between fun and serious activities isn't just about making prompt progress; developing an economical way of life supports your drawn-out prosperity. Recollect that your excursion to monetary significance is a long-distance race, not a run. By dealing with yourself and cultivating a decent way of life, you're establishing the conditions for supported achievement, inventiveness, and satisfaction. As you explore the difficulties and wins ahead, let your obligation to prosperity be a directing power that pushes you toward a future that is both prosperous and agreeable.

Harness the Power of Investments and Passive Income streams.

Here's how to tap into this transformative aspect of your journey:

1. Understand Different Investment Vehicles:
Educate yourself about the various investment options available, such as stocks, bonds, real estate, mutual funds, exchange-traded funds (ETFs), and more. Each comes with its own risk and return profile.

2. Diversify Your Portfolio:
Diversification is a key principle in investing. Spread your investments across different asset classes to minimize risk. A well-diversified portfolio can help cushion the impact of market fluctuations.

3. Set Clear Investment goals:
Define your investment goals—whether it's retirement, buying a home, funding education, or achieving financial independence. Having specific goals guides your investment decisions.

4. Invest for the Long Term:
Investing is a long-term strategy. Avoid making impulsive decisions based on short-term market

fluctuations. Patience and a focus on your long-term objectives are essential.

5. Embrace the Power of Compounding:
Compounding is the magic of earning returns on your initial investment as well as on the returns themselves. The longer your money remains invested, the greater its potential to compound.

6. Consider Passive Index funds:
Passive index funds, or ETFs, are investment vehicles that track a specific market index. They offer diversification, low fees, and the potential for steady, long-term growth.

7. Explore Real Estate Investments:
Real estate can provide both rental income and potential appreciation. Whether residential or commercial, real estate can be a lucrative addition to your investment portfolio.

8. Create Multiple Income Streams:
Passive income streams can come from various sources—dividends, rental income, interest from bonds, royalties from creative works, and more. Aim to create multiple sources of passive income.

9. Start Early and Be consistent:

The power of investments grows with time. Start investing early and contribute consistently to your investment accounts. Regular contributions capitalize on dollar-cost averaging.

10. Rebalance Periodically:
As your investments grow, their proportions within your portfolio may change. Periodically rebalance to ensure your portfolio aligns with your risk tolerance and investment goals.

11. Automated Investments:
Set up automated contributions to your investment accounts. This ensures consistent contributions without the need for constant manual adjustments.

12. Continuously Educate Yourself:
The investment landscape evolves. Stay updated on market trends, economic indicators, and investment strategies. Continuous learning equips you to make informed decisions.

Harnessing investments and passive income streams is a pivotal step toward financial freedom. It transforms your money from a mere tool for transactions into a mechanism for generating wealth and stability. By making well-informed choices, diversifying your portfolio, and maintaining a long-term perspective, you're laying the groundwork for a future that's financially secure and abundant. Remember that every dollar invested is a step toward your financial goals, and each passive income stream you create is a testament to your commitment to living life on your terms.

Reward Society and Leave an Enduring Positive impact.

Genuine significance isn't exclusively estimated by privately invested money; it's additionally about the effect you have on your general surroundings. Rewarding society and leaving a positive inheritance is a strong method for raising your excursion to monetary significance. This is the way you can have a significant effect:

1. Develop a Feeling of philanthropy:
Generosity is the purposeful demonstration of providing to further the prosperity of others. Foster a mentality that values offering in return and adding to causes that align with your qualities.

2. Characterize Your Areas of Impact:
Recognize causes or issues that impact you. Whether it's schooling, medical services, destitution easing, ecological protection, or civil rights, center around regions that profoundly make a difference to you.

3. Set Giving goals:
Similarly, as you put forth monetary and professional objectives, put forth giving objectives. Decide the amount you need to contribute, which associations you need to help, and the effect you intend to accomplish.

4. Volunteer Your Time and skills:

Contributing your time and aptitude can be just as significant as monetary gifts. Volunteer for nearby philanthropies, guide yearning people, or offer free types of assistance in your field.

5. Integrate Surrendering into Your lifestyle:
Coordinate surrendering with your daily schedule. Designate a level of your pay or benefits for beneficent gifts. This reliable responsibility guarantees a positive effect.

6. Support Socially Capable businesses:
Decide to help organizations that focus on friendly and ecological obligations. Thusly, you intensify your effect through your buying choices.

7. Lay out an Establishment or fund:
Consider making a magnanimous establishment or providing a subsidy to formalize your generous endeavors. This design empowers you to oversee and dispense gifts in a calculated manner.

8. Team up with others:
A joint effort increases influence. Collaborate with similar people, associations, or organizations to enhance your aggregate endeavors.

9. Measure and Observe Impact:
Routinely evaluate the effect of your giving. Praise the positive results and learn from the difficulties to refine your methodology.

10. Leave a Heritage Through Endowments:
Consider leaving an enduring legacy by blessing finances that will keep on supporting the things dear to your heart even after your lifetime.

11. Advocate for Change:
Utilize your leverage to advocate for foundational change in regions you care about. Take part in discussions, bring issues to light, and work toward strategy enhancements.

12. Embrace Regular Demonstrations of Kindness:
Little motions can have huge effects. Thoughtful gestures, whether it's aiding a neighbor, supporting a nearby business, or contributing to a local area project, contribute to positive change.

Offering back isn't simply a benevolent demonstration; it's a way to make a superior world for everybody. It's an affirmation that your prosperity is interlaced with the prosperity of the more extensive local area. By directing your assets, impact, and sympathy toward having an effect, you're making an inheritance that reaches a long way beyond private monetary achievements. Keep in mind that the genuine sign of significance isn't simply the abundance you collect, but the positive change you bring to the existence of others and the world in general.